E S T A T E   P U B L I

G000138368

CHICHESTER · BOGN(

BOSHAM · EAST & WEST WITTERING · MIDDL_ . JN · SELSEY

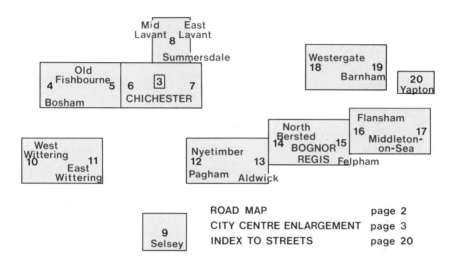

Mid East
Lavant Lavant
8
Summersdale

Old
Fishbourne
4   5   6   3   7
Bosham
CHICHESTER

Westergate
18   19
Barnham
20
Yapton

Flansham
16   17
North
Bersted
14   BOGNOR 15   Middleton-
on-Sea
Nyetimber
12   13   REGIS Felpham
Pagham   Aldwick

West
Wittering
10   11
East
Wittering

9
Selsey

ROAD MAP   page 2
CITY CENTRE ENLARGEMENT   page 3
INDEX TO STREETS   page 20

One-way street	→
Pedestrianized	▨
Car Park	P
Post Office	●
Public Convenience	C
Place of worship	+
Scale of street plans: 4 inches to 1 mile	

Street plans prepared and published by ESTATE PUBLICATIONS, Bridewell House, Tenterden, Kent and based upon the ORDNANCE SURVEY maps with the sanction of the controller of H.M. Stationery Office.

The publishers acknowledge the co-operation of Chichester and Arun district councils in the preparation of these maps.

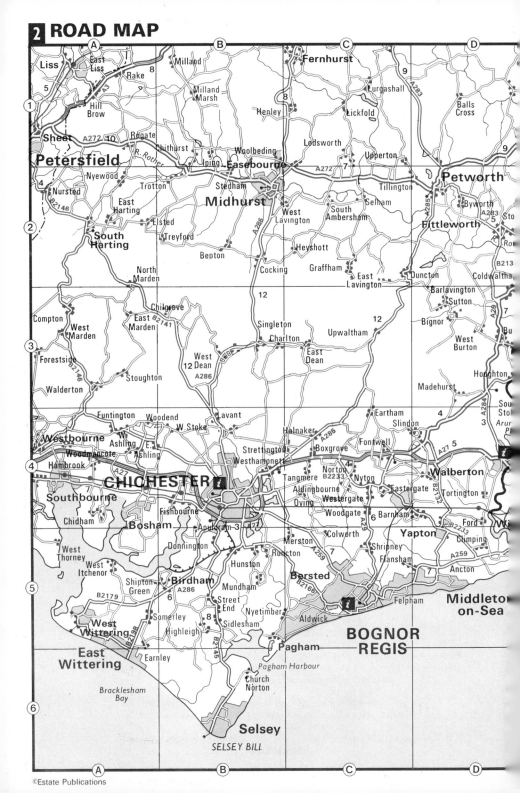

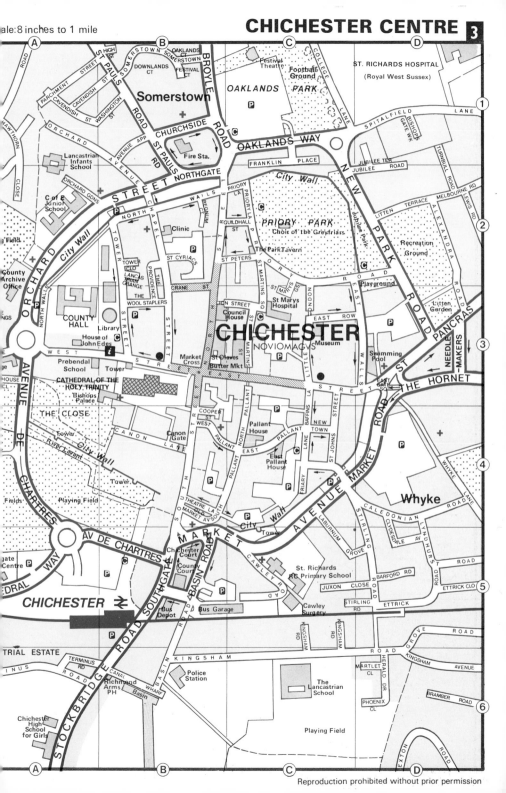

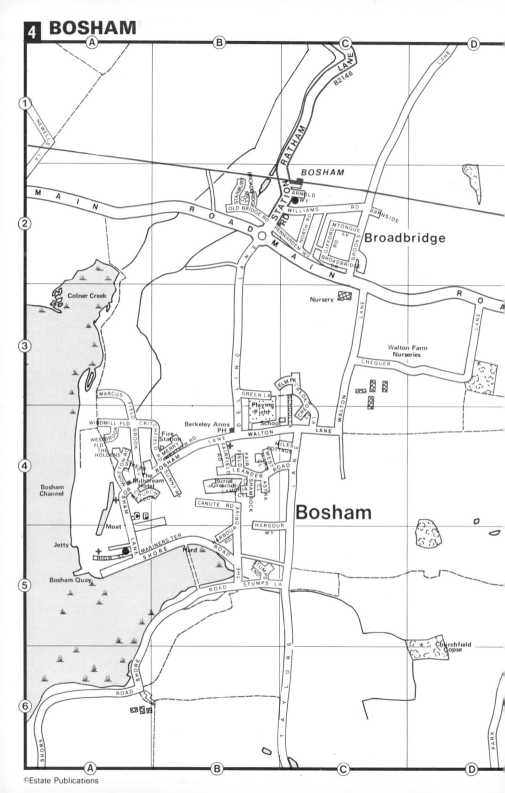

4 BOSHAM

BOSHAM

Broadbridge

Bosham

Colner Creek

Nursery

Walton Farm
Nurseries

Bosham
Channel

Jetty

Bosham Quay

Moat

The
Millstream
Hotel

Berkeley Arms
PH

Fire
Station

Playing
Field

School

Burial
Ground

Churchfield
Copse

Hard

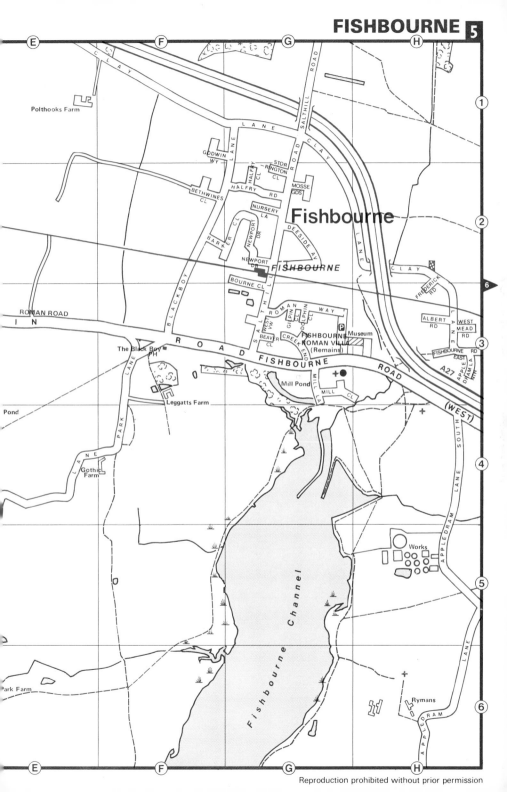

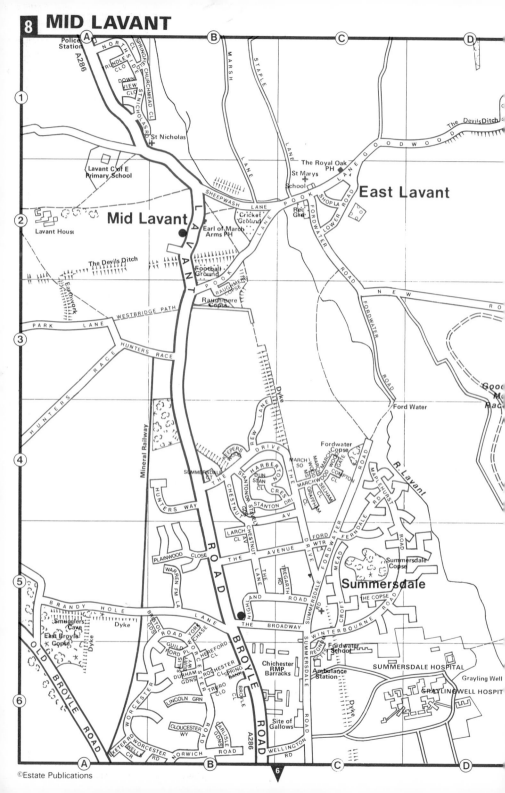

East Beach

Selsey Bill

SELSEY

Police Station

Lifeboat Station

CHICHESTER STREET

HIGH ROAD

HILLFIELD

Green Lawns Caravan Site

White Horse Caravan Park

Caravan Park

Playing Field

Health Centre

The Manhood School

School

The Star PH

Fishermans Joy PH

Neptune PH

Football Ground

Crablands Park

RONTINS BROADREEDS (Holiday Camp)

Hersee Way

Thorny Dr

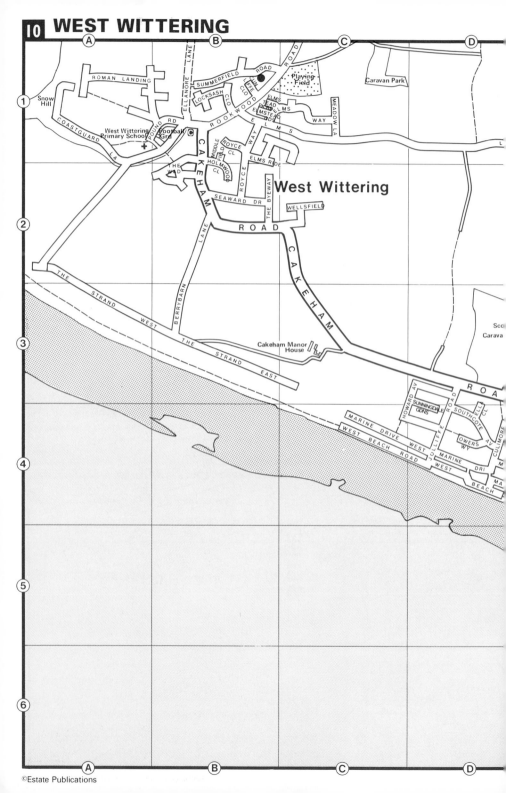

West Wittering

Snow Hill

ROMAN LANDING

ELLANORE LANE

SUMMERFIELD

LOCKSASH CLO

CLO

ROAD

Playing Field

Caravan Park

ELMS MEAD MS

ELMSTEAD

WAY

MEADOW LA

ROOKWOOD RD

West Wittering Primary School

Football Grd

COASTGUARD LA

POUND RD

CAKEHAM

MIDDLE FIELD

ROYCE CL

ELMS RIDE

THE WAD

HOLMWOOD CL

ROYCE WAY

THE BYEWAY

West Wittering

WELLSFIELD

SEAWARD DR

ROAD

CAKEHAM

LANE

THE STRAND

WEST

BERRYBARN LANE

THE STRAND

Cakeham Manor House

Scc
Carava

EAST

ROA

HOWARD AV

SUNNINGDALE GDNS

SOUTHCOTE AV

CL

CULLIMOR

MARINE DRIVE WEST

WEST BEACH ROAD

JOLLIFFE ROAD

TOWERS WY

MARINE WEST DRI

BEACH

MA

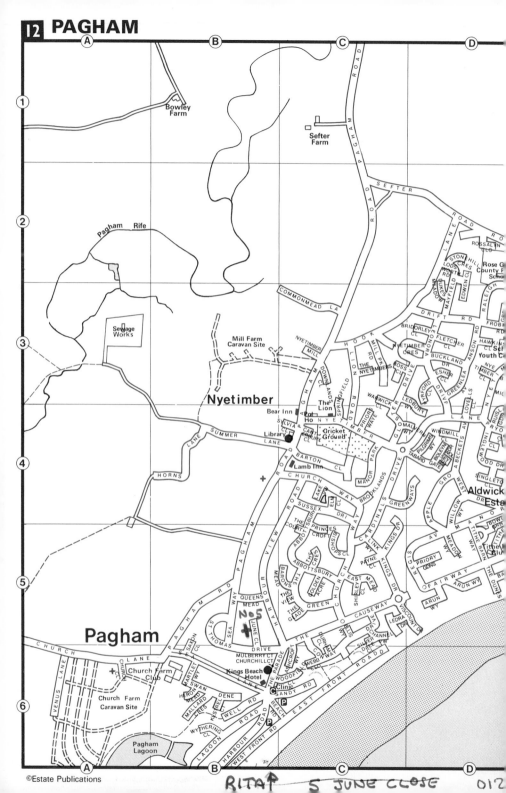

Rita Cripps

6 Mountbatten Court

Belmont Street

Bognor Regis

West Sussex

PO21 - 1JN

Phone 01243
8 25821

Yours sincerely,

Managing Director
UK General Insurance

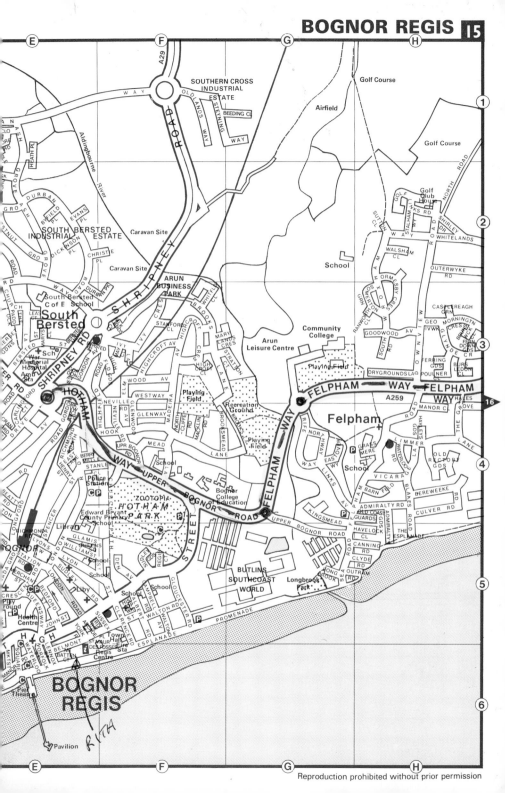

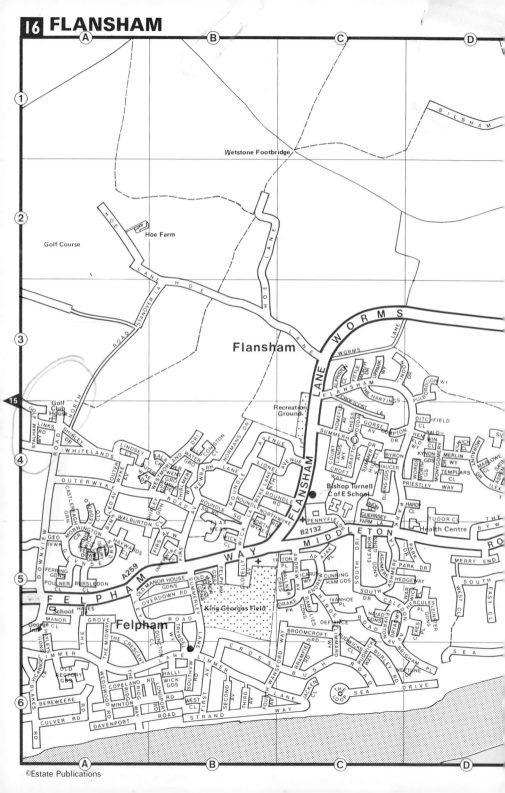

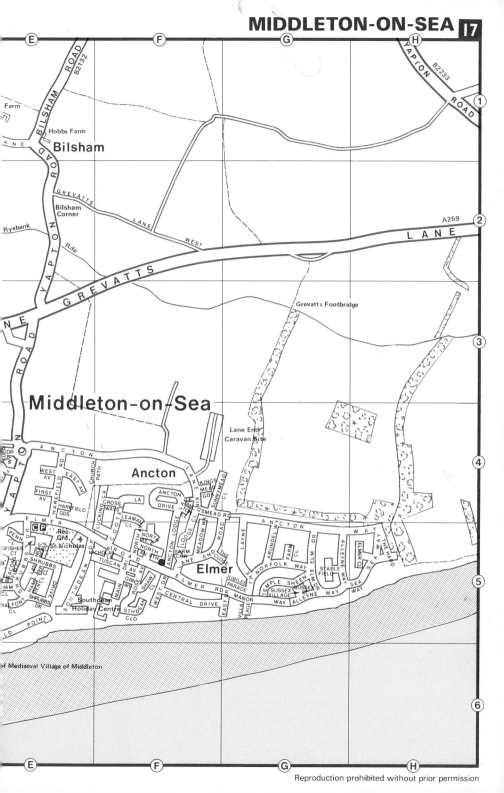

E F G H

1

YAPTON ROAD B2233

BILSHAM ROAD B2132

Farm

Hobbs Farm

Bilsham

GREVATTS

Bilsham
Corner

Ryebank

Rife

LANE WEST

A259 2

L A N E

YAPTON ROAD

GREVATTS

Grevatts Footbridge

3

Middleton-on-Sea

Lane End
Caravan Site

4

YAPTON

ANCTON RD

WEST AV
EAST AV

CHURCH PATH

Ancton

FIRST AV

HAREFIELD GDS

HAREFIELD

LUCKINGS LA

CROSS WAYS

LA

LEAMAN CL

ANCTON DRIVE

ANCTON LODGE LA

KINGS MEAD GDS

SUNNYMEAD CL

KINGSMEAD RD

MEADOW WK

ANCTON

WAY

5

C P
Rec.
Grd.
St. Nicholas

PENN CL
KINGFISHER CT

SHRUBBS

SHRUBBS DR

HAMPENCIL CL

HALFONT CL

SHRUBBS DR

POINT

ELMER

NICHOLAS CL
NORTH
NORTH PLYTH

TUSCAN CL

STROAD

CROSS RD

SHAW DR

MAIN

SOUTHDEAN DR

STHDEAN CLO

WEST DR

CENTRAL DRIVE

EASTDR

ANCTON LODGE CL

FARM CNR

NORTH END CLOSE

THE LANE
ELMER RD

Elmer

JUBILEE PARADE

ELMER

NORFOLK WAY

VILLAGE

MANOR WAY

ARUNDEL CL

TEMPLE SHEEN
SUSSEX
VILLAGE

SUSSEX WAY

ALLEYNE WAY

FARM CL

STABLE FIELD

ELM DR

ALLEYNE WAY

ELMER CL

SEA WAY

THE MEAD

ALLEYNE WAY

Southdean
Holiday Centre

6

f Mediaeval Village of Middleton

E F G H

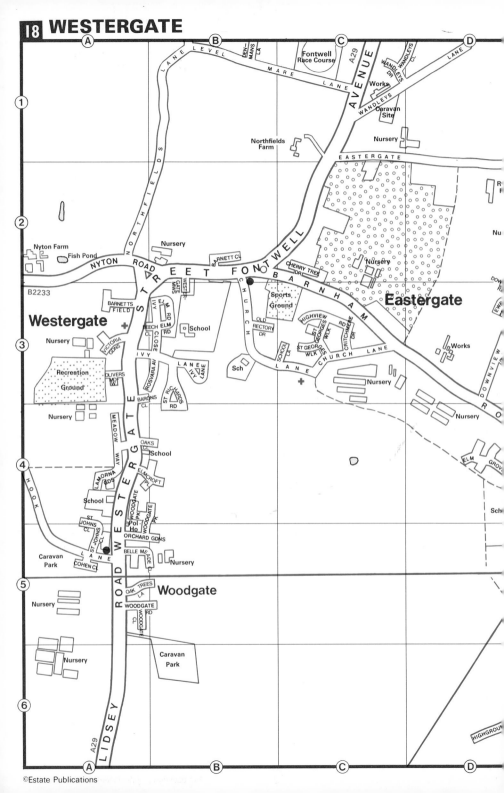

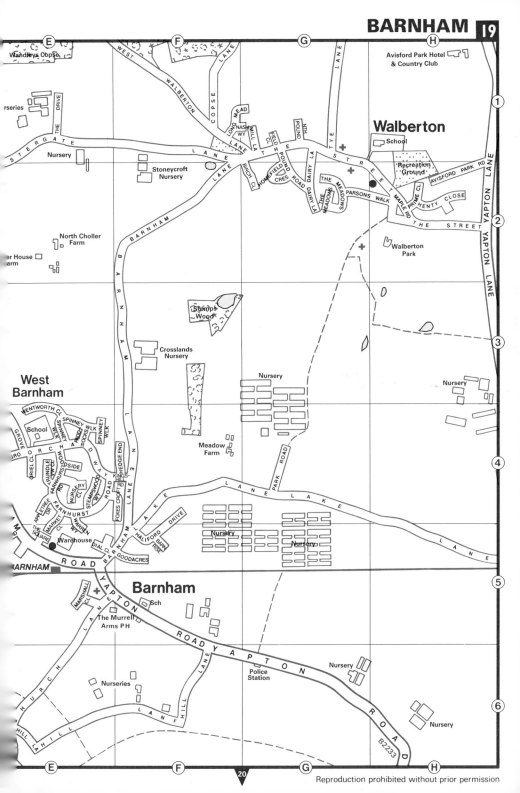

Wandleys Copse

Avisford Park Hotel & Country Club

Walberton

The Drive

WEST WALBERTON LANE

COPSE LANE

TYE LANE

Nursery

School

E STERGATE

Stoneycroft Nursery

LONG MEAD

NASH WY

MILL LA

FIELD

POUND

THE STREET

Recreation Ground

AVISFORD PARK RD

YAPTON LANE

North Choller Farm

BARNHAM LANE

BIRCH CL

HOMEFIELD CRES

POUND ROAD

DAIRY LA

DAIRY LA

THE MEADOWS

PARSONS WALK

THE MEADOWS

PRIME CL

HENTY CLOSE

MAPLE RD

er House arm

Walberton Park

THE STREET

Stemps Wood

Crosslands Nursery

Nursery

Nursery

West Barnham

WENTWORTH CL

SPINNEY WLK

SPINNEY WLK

School

GROVE

ORIEL CL

ORCHARD

FARNHURST RD

ARUNDEL DR

ROOKS CL

WOODSIDE

KINGS WAY

HEDGE END

Meadow Farm

Nursery

PARK ROAD

LANE

LAKE

APPLETREE DR

NURSERY CL

STEMPSWOOD WY

WARREN CL

MARKET CL

THE SQUARE

FARNHURST RD

FOXES CROFT

ROAD

KINGS CL

DIAL LANE

GOODACRES

Warehouse

BARNHAM LAKE LANE

HALIFORD DRIVE

BARN RISE

Nursery

Nursery

LANE LAKE LANE

BARNHAM ROAD

Barnham

MARSHALL CL

YAPTON LANE

Sch

The Murrell Arms PH

CHURCH HILL LA

YAPTON ROAD

YAPTON

Police Station

Nursery

Nurseries

LANE HILL

ROAD

B2233

Nursery

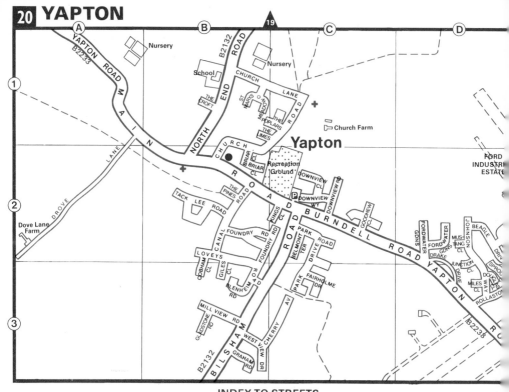

INDEX TO STREETS

BOGNOR

A Beckets Av	12 D4
Abbottsbury	12 C5
Acorn End	13 F3
Addison Way	14 D1
Admiralty Gdns	15 H4
Admiralty Rd	15 H4
Aigburth Av	13 E2
Ajax Pl	16 C5
Albert Rd	15 F5
Alborough Way	13 F3
Aldbourne Dri	13 F4
Alder Way	17 E4
Aldwick Av	14 B6
Aldwick Felds	14 A5
Aldwick Gdns	14 B5
Aldwick Pl	14 B6
Aldwick Rd	14 A5
Aldwick St	14 A6
Alexander Clo	13 F3
Alfriston Clo	16 C3
Alleyne Way	17 G5
Alperton Clo	12 D4
Amberley Dri	14 B4
Ambleside Clo	16 B4
Ancton Clo	17 F4
Ancton Dri	17 F4
Ancton La	17 E4
Ancton Lodge La	17 F5
Ancton Way	17 G4
Andrew Av	16 C5
Annadale Av	15 E4
Anson Rd	12 D3
Apple Gro	12 D4
Argyle Rd	15 E5
Arnhem Rd	14 D3
Arun Rd	14 B4
Arun Way	12 D5
Arundel Way	17 G5
Ash Gro	15 E1
Ashcroft Way	12 C6
Ashmere Gdns	16 C5
Ashmere La	16 C5
Ashurst Clo	14 B2
Aspen Way	16 D4
Avon Clo	16 C4
Bala Cres	16 B4
Baldwin Clo	16 D4

Balliol Clo	14 A4
Balmoral Clo	13 F3
Bank View Clo	14 E4
Barn Feld	15 H4
Barons Mead	12 C5
Barrack La	13 E4
Barton Clo	12 C4
Barton Rd	14 C1
Bartons La	14 C1
Bassett Rd	14 D5
Bay Walk	12 D5
Beach Clo	13 E5
Beach Rd	12 B6
Beaconsfield Clo	17 E5
Beatty Rd	15 E4
Bedenscroft	14 B5
Bedford Av	14 B2
Bedford St	15 E5
Beeding Clo	15 G1
Bell Ct	13 E3
Belmont St	15 E6
Bereweeke Rd	15 H4
Berghstede Rd	14 D2
Berry La	14 C1
Berry Mill Clo	15 E4
Bersted Green Ct	14 D2
Bersted Mews	15 E3
Bersted St	15 E3
Bickleys Ct	14 C6
Bilsham La	16 D1
Bilsham Rd	17 E1
Binsted Av	16 A5
Birch Clo	13 F2
Birdham Clo	14 B3
Bishops Clo	12 C5
Blakemyle	13 G3
Blakes Rd	15 H4
Blenheim Ct	14 A4
Blondell Dri	13 E3
Bowling Green Clo	12 D4
Boxgrove Gdns	13 E3
Bradlond Clo	14 C5
Braemar Way	14 B1
Bramber Clo	14 B4
Bramfield Rd	16 C6
Bramley Gdns	14 D1
Brazwick Av	14 B1
Brent Rd	14 C4
Bridorley Clo	12 D3

Brigham Pl	16 C6
Bronze Clo	15 E1
Brook Clo	14 B4
Brooklands	12 C4
Brooks La	15 F3
Brooksmead	15 F4
Broomcroft Rd	16 C5
Brunswick Clo	15 H3
Buckland Dri	12 D3
Bucknor Clo	12 D3
Bucksham Av	14 B1
Burchett Walk	14 B3
Burley Rd	16 C6
Burngreave Ct	14 C5
Burnham Av	14 D5
Burnham Gdns	14 D5
Burns Gdns	16 C4
Bursledon Clo	16 A5
Byfield Pl	15 E2
Byron Clo	16 C4
Caledon Av	16 C5
Cambridge Dri	14 B4
Cambridge Walk	14 B4
Campbell Rd	15 F5
Canada Gro	15 E5
Canning Rd	15 H5
Cannons Clo	13 E4
Canterbury Clo	12 C4
Cardinals Dri	12 C5
Carlingford Ct	15 E4
Carlton Av	12 D3
Carousel Ct	14 D3
Castlereagh Grn	16 A4
Cavendish Rd	14 D5
Cedar Clo	13 F2
Cedar Clo East	13 F2
Central Av	14 B2
Central Dri, Elmer	17 F5
Central Dri, Nth Bersted	14 B2
Ceres Pl	16 D5
Chalcraft La	14 A4
Chalfont Clo	17 E5
Channel Vw	12 C5
Chapel St	15 E5
Charlwood St	14 D6
Charnwood Rd	14 C2
Chaucer Way	16 C4
Chawkmare Coppice	14 A6

Cherry Clo	13 F3
Chesswood Av	16 C4
Chestnut Gro	15 E2
Cheverley Gdns	13 F3
Chichester Rd	14 B1
Chipley Ct	14 C4
Christchurch Cres	14 A5
Christie Pl	15 E2
Church Clo	12 A6
Church La, Pagham	12 A6
Church La, Sth Bersted	15 E3
Church Path Ancton	17 E4
Church Path, Bognor	15 F4
Church Way	12 C4
Churchill Av	14 A4
Churchill Walk	12 B6
Clarence Rd	15 F5
Clifton Rd	15 E4
Clovelly Av	16 B5
Clyde Rd	15 H5
Clydesdale Gdns	14 C1
College Clo	14 B4
Collyer Av	14 C3
Colts Bay	13 E4
Commonmead La	12 C3
Compton Dri	16 C4
Coniston Clo	16 B4
Conway Dri	12 C6
Cootes La	17 F5
Copeland Rd	16 A6
Copthorne Way	13 E1
Corbishley Rd	14 D2
Cottage Clo	12 D3
Countisbury Clo	14 B5
Courtlands Way	16 C4
Coventry Clo	13 F2
Craigweil La	13 F4
Craigweil Manor	13 E4
Cranford Gdns	15 E4
Crescent Rd	15 E5
Crescent Walk	14 C5
Croft Way	14 C4
Croftcost La	16 C3
Cross Bush Rd	16 B6
Crossways	17 F4
Culver Rd	15 H4
Cunningham Gdns	16 C5
Curlescroft	13 G3
Cygnet Walk	14 D1
Cypress Way	13 E4

ark La	14 A6
avenport Rd	16 A6
avids Clo	14 B3
efiance Pl	16 C5
en Av	15 F5
enham Clo	17 E5
ensihale	14 B5
erwent Gro	16 B4
evonshire Pl	14 D5
evonshire Rd	14 D5
ckinson Pl	15 E2
tchfield Clo	16 D4
orset Rd	14 D3
ove Ct	14 C3
owning Clo	14 A4
ownlands Clo	12 C3
ownview Rd	15 H3
ake Park	16 C5
rift Rd	12 D3
yad Way	16 C5
ygrounds La	15 H3
ukes Meadow	12 D3
uncton Clo	16 B5
urban Park	15 E3
urban Rd	15 E2
urham Clo	12 C5
urlston Dri	14 D2
ast Av	17 E4
ast Clo	16 D5
ast Gro	17 G5
ast Front Rd	12 C6
ast Lake	15 E4
ast Mead	12 C5
astover Way	15 G4
dinburgh Clo	13 F3
dwen Clo	12 D2
bridge Cres	13 E4
eanor Gdns	16 C5
fin Gro	14 D5
izabeth Av	13 E1
izabeth Clo	13 E2
lasdale Rd	14 D5
lis Way	12 C5
m Clo	12 C4
m Dri	17 G5
m Gro	14 C5
mer Clo	17 H5
mer Rd	17 F5
mwood Av	15 F3
y Gdns	13 F2
sher Clo	12 D3
ssex Rd	14 D3
ton Clo	14 A4
vans Pl	15 E2
xeter Clo	14 B5
airlands	14 C2
airway	12 D5
alklands Clo	15 F3
aresmead	14 B6
arm Clo	17 G5
arm Cnr	17 F5
elpham Gdns	16 B5
elpham Rd	15 H4
elpham Way	15 G4
erndown Gdns	16 A5
ernhurst Gdns	13 E3
erring Gdns	16 A5
nch Gdns	14 D1
ndon Dri	16 C3
rs Av	16 B5
rs Av West	16 B5
irst Av, Felpham	16 B6
irst Av, Middleton-on-Sea	17 E4
sh La	14 B6
shermans Walk	13 E4
ttleworth Dri	16 C3
tzwilliam Clo	14 B4
lansham La	16 C4
lansham Park	16 C3
lax Mean	16 B5
letcher Clo	12 D3
ollett Clo	13 F4
ourth Av	16 B6
randor Rd	14 B3
riary Clo	16 D4
rith Rd	14 C4
robisher Rd	12 D3
ursefeld	14 C6
ainsboro Rd	15 E5
arden Ct	13 G3
eorge IV Walk	16 A5
ilwynes	14 B5
ilamis St	15 E5
lencathra Rd	14 D5
lenelg Clo	14 B2
lenway	15 F4
lenwood Av	15 F4

Gloster Dri	12 C4
Gloucester Rd	15 F5
Glynde Cres	16 A5
Godman Clo	13 E3
Golden Acre	12 C5
Golf Links Rd	15 H2
Goodwood Av	15 H3
Gordon Av	15 E4
Gordon Av West	15 E3
Gorse Av	16 C4
Gossamer La	13 E2
Grafton Av	16 C4
Grange Ct	13 G4
Grangefield Way	13 F4
Grangewood Dri	13 F3
Grassmere Clo	15 H4
Gravits La	14 C3
Green Rd	13 E2
Green Way	17 F5
Greencourt Dri	14 B2
Greenlea Av	12 D3
Greenways	12 C4
Greenwood Av	14 D2
Greenwood Clo	14 D2
Grevatts La	17 E3
Grevatts Lane West	17 E2
Greyfriars Clo	14 B5
Greynville Clo	12 D3
Greystone Av	14 B1
Grosvenor Gdns	13 E2
Grosvenor Way	13 E2
Guernsey Farm La	16 C4
Gunwin Ct	13 E3
Hadley Clo	17 E4
Hales FP	15 H3
Halliwick Gdns	16 B6
Halnaker Gdns	13 E3
Hambledon Pl	14 D5
Hamilton Gdns	13 F4
Hampden Clo	17 E5
Hampshire Av	14 C3
Hampton Ct	14 B4
Harbour Rd	12 B6
Harbour View Rd	12 B5
Hardy Clo	16 D4
Harefield Gdns	17 E4
Harefield Rd	17 E4
Hastings Clo	14 B4
Hatherleigh Clo	14 C3
Hatherleigh Gdns	14 C3
Havelock Clo	15 H5
Havelock Rd	15 E4
Hawkins Clo	13 D3
Hawks Pl	14 D1
Hawthorn Rd	14 B5
Haydon Clo	13 E4
Hayleys Gdns	15 H4
Haywards Clo	16 A5
Hazel Gro	13 E2
Hazel Rd	14 D2
Heath Pl	15 E1
Hechle Wood	14 A6
Hedgeway	16 C5
Heghbrok Way	14 C6
Henfield Way	16 D4
Henry St	15 E4
Hercules Pl	16 D5
Heron Clo	14 D1
Heron Mead	12 B6
Hertford Clo	14 A4
Heston Gro	13 E4
Hewarts La	13 E2
High St	15 E5
High Trees	14 B6
Highcroft Av	15 F3
Highcroft Clo	15 F3
Highcroft Cres	15 F3
Highfield Gdns	15 F3
Highfield Rd	15 F4
Highgate Dri	14 B1
Highland Av	14 D4
Hillsboro Rd	14 D4
Hinde Rd	16 C5
Hislop Walk	15 F5
Hoe La	16 B3
Holland Clo	14 B3
Holly Ct	15 E2
Homefield	16 C4
Homing Gdns	14 C1
Hook La, Bognor Regis	15 F4
Hook La, Nyetimber	12 C3
Hornbeam Clo	14 B6
Horns La	12 B4
Hotham Way	15 E4
Howard House	14 C4
Hughes Clo	14 B4
Hunters Clo	13 E4
Icarus Way	16 C5
Ilex Way	17 E4
INDUSTRIAL ESTATES:	
Arun Bus. Park	15 F2

South Bersted Ind Est	15 E2
Inglewood Clo	12 D4
Inglewood Dri	12 D4
Innerwyke Clo	16 B5
Ivanhoe Pl	16 C5
Ivy Cres	15 F3
Ivy La	15 F3
Ivydale Rd	14 C4
Jacken Clo	16 C6
John St	15 E5
Jubilee Par	17 G5
June Clo	12 B5
Juniper Clo	17 E4
Keats Walk	14 C5
Keble Clo	14 B5
Kenilworth Rd	14 C4
Kenlegh	13 G3
Kestrel Ct	12 B6
Kew Gdns	14 B3
Kilwich Clo	16 D4
King George Ct	14 C3
Kingfisher Ct	17 E5
Kings Dri	12 C5
Kings Par	14 C6
Kingsmead	15 G4
Kingsmead Gdns	17 F4
Kingsmead Rd	17 F4
Kingsway	13 F4
Kynon Gdns	16 D4
Kyoto Ct	14 C5
Laburnum Gro	14 D2
Lagoon Rd	12 B6
Lake View	12 C4
Lane End Rd	17 F5
Langley Gro	12 D4
Larch Clo	15 E1
Larchfield Clo	13 F4
Latiter Clo	17 E5
Laurel Gro	15 E2
Leaman Clo	17 F4
Leas Ct	15 E3
Ledbury Way	12 C3
Ledra Dri	12 C5
Leecroft	14 A6
Leinster Gdns	16 D5
Lennox St	15 E6
Leonora Dri	12 D3
Leopold Clo	16 A4
Leverton Av	16 C5
Lewes Clo	14 B4
Ley Rd	16 A5
Lichfield Gdn	13 F3
Lilac Clo	17 E4
Limmard Way	16 C6
Limmer La	16 A3
Lincoln Av	13 E2
Linden Ct	15 E4
Linden Rd	14 D4
Lindsey Ct	16 A4
Link Way	12 C5
Links Av	15 G4
Lion Rd	12 C3
Lionel Av	16 B4
Little Babbsham	14 A6
Loats La	14 B1
Lodge Clo	17 F5
Lodge Ct	13 G3
Lodsworth Rd	12 D2
London Rd	15 E5
Longbrook	15 G5
Longford Rd	15 E5
Longport Rd	16 B6
Lovells Clo	12 D3
Lower Bognor Rd	14 A4
Lucerne Av	13 F3
Lucking La	17 F4
Ludlow Clo	13 F3
Lyon St	15 E5
Lyon St West	15 E5
Macklin Rd	15 E4
Madeira Av	15 F4
Main Dri	17 F5
Mallard Cres	12 B6
Malmayne Ct	14 A5
Malvern Way	12 C4
Manet Sq	14 C2
Manor Clo	15 H4
Manor Par	15 E5
Manor Park	12 C4
Manor Way, Aldwick Bay	12 D4
Manor Way, Elmer	17 G5
Mansfield Rd	14 D3
Maple Clo	16 D4
Maple Gdns	15 E1
Margaret Clo	14 C6
Marine Dri West	14 C6
Marine Par	14 D6
Market St	15 E6

Markfield	14 D1
Marlborough Ct	14 B3
Marlowe Clo	16 D4
Marshall Av	14 D4
Martlet Way	12 B6
Marylands Cres	15 F3
Mauldmare Clo	14 B6
May Clo	15 F3
Mayfield	12 D3
Mayfield Rd	14 C4
Mead La	15 F4
Meadow Walk	17 F5
Meadow Way, Aldwick Bay Est	12 D5
Meadow Way, Nth Bersted	14 C2
Merchant St	15 E5
Merlin Way	16 D4
Merrion Av	14 D3
Merry End	16 D5
Merton Clo	14 A4
Micklam Clo	12 D3
Middleton Rd	16 C5
Mill Park Rd	12 C3
Minton Rd	16 A6
Mons Av	14 D3
Montgomery Dri	16 D4
Moorhen Way	14 D2
Moraunt Dri	16 D4
Mornington Cres	16 A5
Mountbatten Ct	15 E6
Mulberry Ct	12 B6
Murina Av	14 D3
Naiad Gdns	16 C5
Nelson Rd	14 C5
Neptune Ct	16 D6
Neville Rd	15 F4
Newbarn La, Flansham	16 B4
Newbarn La, Nth Bersted	14 B1
Newhall Clo	14 B5
Newtown Av	14 B2
Nightingale Ct	17 E5
Norbren Av	14 C3
Norfolk Clo	14 D6
Norfolk Sq	14 D6
Norfolk St	15 E6
Norfolk Way	17 G5
Normans Dri	16 B4
Normanton Av	14 D5
North Av	17 F5
North Av East	17 F5
North Av South	17 F5
North Bersted St	14 C1
North Rd	16 A4
Northcliffe Rd	15 F4
Northcote Rd	14 C4
Northway	15 G4
Northwyke Clo	16 B5
Northwyke Rd	16 B5
Nuffield Clo	14 A4
Nyetimber Clo	12 D3
Nyetimber Cres	12 D3
Nyetimber La	12 D3
Nyetimber Mill	12 C3
Nyewood Gdns	14 D5
Nyewood La	14 C4
Nyewood Pl	14 D6
Oak Clo	14 D2
Oak Gro	15 E2
Oakwood Gdns	15 E4
Ockley Ct	15 E5
Ockley Rd	15 E5
Old Bakery La	14 D6
Old Coastguards	15 H4
Old Farm Clo	13 F3
Old Manor House Gdns	16 A5
Old Pl	13 F3
Old Point	17 E5
Old Rectory Gdns	15 H4
Oldlands Way	15 F1
Orchard Way	14 D3
Ormesby Cres	15 H2
Osprey Clo	14 D1
Outerwyke Av	16 A4
Outerwyke Gdns	16 A4
Outerwyke Rd	16 A4
Outram Rd	15 G5
Overdown Rd	16 A5
Oxford Clo	14 A4
Oxford St	14 D6
Pagham Rd	12 B5
Park Dri	16 D5
Park Rd	14 D6
Park Ter	14 D6
Parkfield Av	13 E2
Parklands Av	14 D4
Parkway	14 C5
Payne Clo	12 C5
Pembroke Way	14 A4

Penn Clo 17 E5
Pennyfields 16 C5
Peterhouse Clo 14 B4
Pevensey Rd 14 B4
Pilgrims Way 12 D4
Pine Walk 13 F2
Pinehurst Pk 13 E1
Place St Maur des Fosses 15 F5
Plover Clo 14 D1
Poulner Clo 16 A5
Priestley Way 16 D5
Princes Croft 12 C5
Princess Av 14 C6
Priors Waye 12 C4
Priory Gdns 12 D5
Promenade 15 F5
Pryors La 12 E4
Pulborough Way 16 D3
Pyrford Clo 12 D3

Queens Fields Walk 14 B4
Queens Fields E 14 B4
Queens Fields W 14 A4
Queens Mead 12 B5
Queens Sq 15 E5
Queensway, Bognor Regis 15 E5
Queensway, Craigweil 13 F4

Radford Rd 14 D3
Raleigh Rd 12 D3
Ramillies Gdns 16 C5
Ranworth Clo 15 H3
Ravens Way 14 D1
Rayscroft Clo 13 G3
Redwood Pl 13 G3
Regents Way 14 B4
Regis Av 12 D5
Regis Ct 15 F5
Renoir Ct 14 C2
Renoir Mews 14 C2
Richmond Av 14 C5
Richmond Avenue Way 14 C5
Richmond Rd 15 E5
Richmond Rd Nth 15 E4
Rife Way 15 G4
Ripon Gdns 13 F2
Robins Dri 13 F2
Rochester Way 13 F3
Rock Gdns 14 D6
Rodney Clo 13 E2
Romney Broad Walk 14 C2
Rose Av 17 F5
Rose Ct 13 E2
Rose Green Rd 12 D2
Ross Clo 12 C3
Rossalyn Clo 12 D2
Roundle Av 16 B4
Roundle Rd 16 B4
Roundle Sq 16 B4
Roundle Sq Rd 16 B4
Rowan Way 14 C1
Rucrofts Clo 14 B5
Rudwicks Clo 16 C6
Rudwicks Way 16 C6
Ruislip Gdns 12 D4
Runnymede Ct 14 B3
Rusbridge Clo 13 F1

Sadler St 15 E6
St Anthonys Walk 13 E3
St Clares Gdns 14 C2
St Johns Clo 14 B4
St Marys Clo 15 E3
St Nicholas La 17 F5
St Peters Clo 14 A4
St Richards Dri 13 F2
St Richards Way 13 F3
St Thomas Dri 12 B5
St Winifreds Clo 14 D5
Salisbury Clo 16 A5
Sandringham Way 14 C4
Sandy Rd 12 B6
Sandymount Av 14 D3
Sandymount Clo 14 D2
Satinwood Clo 16 D4
Saxon Clo 12 B5
Scott Clo 14 D6
Scott St 14 D6
Sea Clo 17 E5
Sea Dri 16 C6
Sea La, Middleton 17 E5
Sea La, Pagham 12 B6
Sea Rd 15 G5
Sea Way, Elmer 17 H5
Sea Way, Middleton-on-Sea 16 D6
Sea Way, Pagham 12 B5
Seacourt Clo 13 F4
Second Av 16 B6
Sefter Rd 12 C2
Sefton Av 13 F2

Selsey Av 14 C6
Selwyn Clo 14 B4
Servite Clo 14 D4
Shaw Clo 17 F5
Shearwater Dri 14 D2
Shelley Rd 14 C5
Sherwood Clo 14 C2
Sherwood Rd 14 C2
Ship Field 14 B6
Shirley Clo 12 C5
Shirley Dri 16 A4
Shirley Gdn 16 B4
Shorecroft 14 B6
Shripney Rd 15 E3
Shrubbs Dri 17 E5
Silver Birch Dri 16 D4
Silverdale Clo 12 C5
Silverston Av 14 C6
Singleton Clo 12 D4
Somerset Gdns 15 E3
Somerton Grn 15 H3
South Av 14 B5
South Dri 16 C5
South Rd 15 H3
South Walk 16 D5
South Way 14 C3
Southdean Clo 17 F5
Southdean Dri 17 E5
Southdown Rd 14 D5
Southover Rd 15 E5
Southview Rd 16 B6
Southwark Walk 13 F2
Spencer St 15 E5
Springfield 12 C4
Stable Field 17 G5
Stalham Way 15 H2
Stanbrok Clo 14 A5
Stanford Clo 15 F3
Stanley Clo 15 E4
Stanmore Gdns 13 F3
Stanover La 16 A3
Stapleton Ct 13 E3
Station Rd 15 E5
Steyne 15 E6
Steyne St 15 E5
Steyning Way 15 F1
Stirling Way 13 F3
Stocker Rd 14 D6
Stoneage Clo 15 E1
Stonehill Cres 12 D2
Stoney Stile Clo 13 E4
Stoney Stile La 13 E4
Strand Way 16 B6
Strange Gdn 13 G4
Stratton Ct 15 G3
Stroud Green Dri 14 B3
Sturges Rd 14 D5
Sudbury Clo 12 D4
Sudley Gdns 15 F5
Sudley Rd 15 E5
Summer La 12 B4
Summerhill Clo 16 C4
Summerhill Dri 16 C4
Summerley La 16 B5
Sun Park Clo 14 B2
Sundale La 16 D4
Sunningdale Gdns 14 D1
Sunnymead Clo 17 F4
Sussex Clo 17 G5
Sussex Dri 12 C4
Sussex Rd 15 F5
Sussex Village 17 G5
Sutherland Clo 14 D5
Sutton Clo 15 H2
Swan Dene 12 B6
Swansea Gdns 14 D6
Sycamore Rd 15 E1
Sylvan Way 14 D5
Sylvia Clo 12 C4

Tabard Gate 12 D4
Tamarisk Clo 15 E2
Tangmere Gdns 13 E3
Templars Clo 16 D4
Temple Sheen 17 G5
Tennyson Rd 14 C5
The Arcade 15 E5
The Avenue 14 D5
The Byeway 12 D5
The Byway 16 D5
The Causeway 12 C5
The Clevets 13 E4
The Close 13 E5
The Close, Elmer 17 F5
The Court 12 C5
The Crescent 12 C5
The Crescent, Felpham 16 A5
The Croft 14 B3
The Dell 14 C2
The Drive 13 E4
The Dunes 12 D5
The Esplanade 15 E6
The Glade 12 C5

The Green 12 C5
The Grove 16 A5
The Hard 17 H5
The Hartings 16 C3
The Hollies 14 B3
The Hopgarton 14 A5
The Lawn 13 F3
The Layne 17 G5
The Loop 16 C6
The Midway 14 A6
The Nyetimbers 12 C3
The Orchard 13 E4
The Orchard Clo 14 D5
The Paddock 15 E3
The Parade 12 B6
The Pound 14 A6
The Precinct 14 B4
The Ridgway 14 A6
The Ridings 13 E4
The Spinney 13 F2
The Thickets 13 E2
The View 12 C5
Third Av 16 B6
Thirlmere Way 16 B4
Thorndene Av 14 D4
Thrusloes 14 B5
Tinghall 14 A5
Tithe Barn Clo 12 D5
Tithe Barn Way 12 D5
Town Cross Av 14 D4
Trendle Grn 14 B5
Trinity Way 14 B4
Triton Pl 16 C5
Trotyn Croft 13 G3
Truro Cres 13 F2
Tryndel Way 16 B5
Tudor Clo 16 D4
Tuscan Av 17 F5
Tyne Way 13 F2

Ullswater Gro 16 B4
Uppark Way 16 C3
Upper Bognor Rd 15 F4
Upper Bognor Rd 15 G4

Valentines Gdns 13 E3
Van Dyke Pl 14 C2
Van Gogh Pl 14 C2
Venus La 12 A6
Vicarage La 15 H4
Victoria Dri 14 D6
Victoria Rd 14 D6
Victoria Rd Sth 14 D6
Villa Plage 17 G5
Viscount Dri 12 C5

Wadhurst Clo 14 D4
Wakefield Way 13 F2
Walburton Clo 16 A4
Wallfield 14 B6
Wallner Cres 16 C5
Walsham Clo 15 H2
Walton Av 15 F5
Walton Rd 15 F5
Wansford Way 16 B6
Warblers Way 14 D1
Warwick Clo 12 C3
Warwick Pl 16 D5
Waterloo Rd 15 H4
Waterloo Sq 15 E6
Watersedge 13 G4
Waverley Rd 14 C4
Webb Clo 12 C6
Wedgwood Rd 14 A6
Well Rd 12 B6
Wellington Rd 14 D5
Wells Cres 13 F2
Wessex Av 14 C6
West Av, Aldwick 14 B5
West Av, Middleton-on-Sea 17 E4
West Clo, Felpham 12 B6
West Clo, Middleton-on-Sea 16 D5
West Dri, Elmer 17 F5
West Dri, Nyetimber 12 D4
West Front Rd 12 B6
West Meads Dri 14 B3
West St 15 E6
Westfield 14 C1
Westingway 14 C5
Westloats Gdns 14 C3
Westloats La 14 C3
Westminster Dri 13 F2
Westmoreland Dri 16 B4
Westway 15 F3
White Knight Av 14 D4
Whitebeam Way 16 D4
Whitelands 16 A4
Whiteways 14 C2
Whiteways Clo 14 C2
Whitfield Clo 15 F3
Wick Clo 16 B5

Wick La 16
William St 15
Willow Way 12
Willowhale Av 13
Willowhale Grn 13
Wilman Gdns 13
Windmill Clo 12
Windsor Clo 14
Winston Clo 14
Winston Cres 14
Wolsey Sq 12
Wood End 14
Wood St 14
Woodfield Clo 12
Woodlands Rd 14
Worcester Clo 14
Wordsworth Gdns 16
Worms La 16
Wren Cres 14
Wroxham Way 15
Wychwood Clo 13
Wychwood Walk 13
Wyde Feld 14
Wyke La Nth 16
Wythering Clo 12

Yapton Rd 17
Yeomans Acre 14
Yew Tree Clo 14
York Rd 15

CHICHESTER

Adelaide Rd 7
Albert Rd 6
Alexandra Rd 3
Appledram Lane Nth 6
Appledram Lane Sth 6
Armadale Rd 7
Arnold Way 4
Ashburnham Clo 6
Astra Clo 4
Avenue App 3
Avenue de Chartres 3

Baffins La 3
Balmoral Rd 7
Barford Rd 3
Barker Clo 5
Barlow Rd 6
Barnfield Dri 7
Barnside 4
Barton Rd 6
Basin Rd 3
Beaver Clo 5
Beech Av 6
Belgrave Cres 6
Bell Clo 6
Bethwines Clo 5
Birdham Rd 6
Bishop Luffa Clo 6
Bishopsgate Walk 3
Blackboy La 5
Blandford Rd 7
Blenheim Gdns 7
Bognor Rd 7
Bosham La 4
Bourne Clo 5
Bradshaw Rd 7
Bramber Rd 3
Brandy Hole La 8
Bride Oake Clo 6
Bridge Rd 7
Bristol Gdns 8
Broadbridge Dri 4
Broadbridge Mill 4
Brook Av 4
Brooks La 4
Broyle Clo 8
Broyle Rd 3
Buckingham Dri 7
Bywater Way 6

Caernarvon Rd 7
Caledonian Rd 3
Cambrai Av 7
Cambria Clo 4
Canal Wharf 3
Canon La 3
Canterbury Clo 6
Canute Rd 4
Carleton Rd 6
Carlisle Gdns 8
Castleman Rd 7
Cathedral Mews 6
Cathedral Way 3
Cavendish St 3
Cawley Rd 3
Cedar Dri 6
Chandler Rd 6
Chapel St 3
Charles Av 7
Chatfield Rd 7

EAST WITTERING/ WEST WITTERING

Elm Clo	11 G5
Elms La	10 B1
Elms Ride	10 B1
Elms Way	10 B1
Elmstead Gdns	10 B1
Elmstead Park Rd	10 B1
Ely Clo	11 E3
Eton Dri	11 E3
Farm Rd	11 G5
Field Rd	11 F4
First Av	11 G6
Fox Warren Clo	11 E3
Furzefield	11 E2
Garden Av	11 G5
Grayswood Av	11 G5
Harmony Dri	11 G5
Harrow Dri	11 E3
Holmwood Clo	10 B1
Howard Av	10 D3
Joliffe Rd	10 D4
Kestral Clo	11 F5
Kimbridge Rd	11 F5
Lacock Clo	11 H6
Legion Way	11 F5
Locksash Clo	10 B1
Longlands Rd	11 E4
Manton Clo	11 H5
Marine Clo	10 D4
Marine Dri	10 D4
Marine Dri West	10 C4
Marineside	11 G6
Meadow La	10 C1
Meadows Rd	11 F4
Middlefield	10 B1
Mill Gdns	11 E3
Nab Walk	11 E5
Northern Cres	11 E3
Oakfield Av	11 E4
Oakfield Rd	11 E4
Owers Way	10 D4
Oxford Clo	11 E3
Peerley Clo	11 F5
Peerley Rd	11 F5
Piggery Hall La	11 E2
Plover Clo	11 G5
Pond Rd	11 G5
Pound Rd	10 B1
Roman Landing	10 A1
Rookwood Rd	10 B1
Royce Clo	10 B1
Royce Way	10 B2
Russell Rd	10 D3
Sandpiper Ct	11 F5
Sandringham Clo	11 G5
Seafield Clo	11 F4
Seafield Way	11 F4
Seafields	11 G6
Seagate Clo	10 D4
Seaward Dri	10 B2
Shalbourne Cres	11 H5
Shingle Walk	11 E5
Shore Rd	11 E4
Shoreside Walk	11 E4
Solent Rd	11 E4
Southcote Av	10 D4
Stocks La	11 E4
Stubcroft La	11 G4
Summerfield Rd	10 B1
Sunningdale Gdns	10 D3
Tamarisk Walk	11 E4
The Byeway	10 B2
The Crescent	10 D4
The Strand East	10 B3
The Strand West	10 A2
The Wad	10 B2
Third Av	11 G6
Tile Barn La	11 H1
Tower Pl	11 E3
Wellsfield	10 C2
Wessex Av	11 F4
West Beach	10 D4
West Beach Rd	10 C4
West Bracklesham Dri	11 F5
Wilton Clo	11 G5
Windsor Dri	11 E3
Woodborough Clo	11 H5
Wyatt Ct	11 E4

SELSEY

Acorn Clo	9 B2
Albion Rd	9 E3
Allandale Clo	9 E2
Arnell Av	9 D3
Beach Gdns	9 C4
Beach Rd	9 E2
Beaufield Clo	9 C4
Beverley Clo	9 E3
Birches Clo	9 B2
Bonnar Clo	9 C3
Bonnar Rd	9 C3
Brampton Clo	9 C3
Bream La	9 A2
Bridle Way	9 C3
Broad View	9 E2
Broomfield Rd	9 E1
Burlington Gdns	9 E3
Byways	9 D4
Chainbridge La	9 A1
Chale Gdns	9 D3
Cherry Gdns	9 C4
Chichester Rd	9 D1
Chichester Way	9 F1
Church Rd	9 D1
Clayton Rd	9 B3
Coach House Clo	9 D2
Colt St	9 B2
Constable Dri	9 E2
Coppice La	9 C2
Cotland Rd	9 E3
Coxes Rd	9 C3
Crablands	9 B2
Crablands Clo	9 C2
Croft Rd	9 C3
Croft Way	9 C2
Danefield Rd	9 B4
Deer Park La	9 A1
Dennys Clo	9 D2
Denshare Rd	9 D1
Drift La	9 B2
Drift Rd	9 E1
East Bank	9 E2
East Beach Rd	9 E2
East St	9 C2
East Way	9 E2
Eels Cross	9 A1
Elm Gro	9 C3
Elm Tree Clo	9 D2
Elmsfield	9 D2
Fish La	9 A1
Fishermans Walk	9 E3
Fontwell Rd	9 E2
Fraser Clo	9 E3
Freeways	9 B1
Gainsborough Dri	9 D2
Gillway	9 F1
Glen Cres	9 D2
Grafton Rd	9 D4
Grant Clo	9 C2
Green La	9 C3
Grove Rd	9 D3
Hanover Clo	9 E2
Harcourt Way	9 E1
Heron Clo	9 A1
Hersee Way	9 B3
High St	9 C2
Hillfield Rd	9 C4
Holford Grn	9 E2
Horsefield Rd	9 C2
Island La	9 A1
Island Loop	9 A1
James St	9 D3
Kilnwood Clo	9 E2
Kings Ct	9 D1
Kingsway	9 E3
Landseer Dri	9 E2
Langton Clo	9 C3
Large Acres	9 C2
Latham Rd	9 C3
Lewis Rd	9 C2
Lingfield Way	9 E2
Littlefield Clo	9 E2
Lobster La	9 A1
Longacre	9 C3
Longacre La	9 C4
Mackerel La	9 A1
Magpie La	9 A1
Malden Way	9 C2
Malthouse Rd	9 D2
Manor Farm Clo	9 D1
Manor Farm Ct	9 D1
Manor La	9 E2
Manor Rd	9 D3
Marine Dri	9 E2
Marine Gdns	9 C4
Marisfield Pl	9 E2
Meadowland	9 C3
Medmerry	9 A2
Merryfield Dri	9 E2
Montalan Cres	9 A2
Mountwood Rd	9 E1
Murray Rd	9 C3
Nab Tower La	9 A1
Netherton Clo	9 D2
Newfield Rd	9 F1
North Rd	9 D2
Northfield	9 E2
Orchard Av	9 D3
Orpen Pl	9 E2
Otard Clo	9 D3
Paddock La	9 C2
Park Av	9 E2
Park Cres	9 F1
Park La	9 F1
Park Rd	9 F1
Peachey Rd	9 C3
Prawn Clo	9 B1
Rife La	9 A1
Robins Clo	9 D2
Romney Garth	9 E2
Round Piece	9 B1
Roundpiece La	9 A2
Roundstone Way	9 E1
Ruskin Clo	9 E3
Saddle La	9 C2
St Georges Clo	9 E1
St Hildas Clo	9 C3
St Itha Clo	9 D3
St Itha Rd	9 D3
St Peters Cres	9 D1
St Wilfreds Clo	9 F1
Sandy Point	9 A1
School La	9 C2
Seagull Clo	9 A1
Seal Rd	9 C4
Seal Sq	9 C4
Seaview Ct	9 C4
Sherbourne La	9 A1
Slattsfield Clo	9 E2
Solent Way	9 C4
Southern Rd	9 D4
Sunnymead Clo	9 D3
Sunnymead Dri	9 D3
The Bridgeway	9 C3
The Causeway	9 A2
The Close	9 F2
The Horseshoe	9 C2
The Oval	9 D4
The Wadeway	9 B2
The Willows	9 D1
Thorny Dri	9 B3
Tretawn Gdns	9 E3
Turner Way	9 E2
Tythe Barn Rd	9 D4
Ursula Av	9 C3
Ursula Av Nth	9 C3
Ursula Sq	9 C4
Vincent Rd	9 B3
Warner Rd	9 A3
Warners La	9 B1
Wellington Gdns	9 D2
West Sands La	9 B2
West St	9 B3
Western Rd	9 D3
Wheatfield Rd	9 E1
Widgeon Clo	9 A1
Windsor Rd	9 D3
Woodland Rd	9 C4
York Rd	9 D4

WESTERGATE/ BARNHAM

Appletree Dri	19 E4
Avisford Park Rd	19 H2
Barn Rise	19 F5
Barnett Clo	18 B2
Barnetts Field	18 A3
Barnham La	19 F2
Barnham Rd, Barnham	19 E4
Barnham Rd, Westergate	18 C2
Barons Clo	18 A3
Beech Clo	18 B3
Belle Meade Clo	18 A5
Birch Clo	19 G2
Cherry Tree Dri	18 C2
Church La, Barnham	19 E6
Church La, Eastergate	18 B3
Cohen Clo	18 A5
Copse La	19 F1
Critchmere Dri	18 C3
Dairy La	19 G2
Denmans La	18 B1
Dial Clo	19 E5
Downview Rd	18 D3
Eastergate La	18 C1
Elm Gro	18 D3
Elm Grove Sth	18 D4
Elm Rd	18 B3
Elmcroft Pl	18 A4
Ewens Gdns	18 D3
Farnhurst Rd	19 E4
Field Clo	19 G1
Fontwell Av	18 B2
Foxes Croft	19 F4
Goodacres	19 F5
Gospond Rd	19 E5
Halford Clo	19 F5
Hedge End	19 F4
Henty Clo	19 H2
Highground La	19 E6
Highview Rd	18 C3
Hill La	19 E6
Homefield Cres	19 G2
Hook La	18 A4
Ivy Clo	18 B3
Ivy La	18 A3
Lake La	19
Lamorna Gdns	18 A
Level Mare La	18 B
Lidsey Rd	18 A
Long Mead	19
Maple Rd	19
Market Clo	19 E
Marshall Clo	19 E
Meadow Way	18 A
Mill La	19 C
Nash Way	19
North Pound	19 C
Northfield La	18 A
Nursery Clo	19 E
Nyton Rd	18 A
Oak Clo	18 A
Oak Trees La	18 A
Old Rectory Dri	18 E
Olivers Meadow	18 A
Orchard Gdns	18 A
Orchard Way	19 E
Oriel Clo	19 E
Paddocks	19 E
Park Rd	19 C
Parsons Walk	19 C
Pound Rd	19 C
Prime Clo	19 H
Rosvara Av	18 E
St Georges Walk	18 C
St Johns Clo	18 A
St Richards Rd	18 E
School La	18 C
Spinney Walk	19 E
Stempswood Way	19 E
The Meadows	19 C
The Drive	19 E
The Square	19 E
The Street	19 C
Trundle View Clo	19 E
Tye La	19 C
Victoria Gdns	18 A
Wandleys Clo	18 C
Wandleys Dri	18 C
Wandleys La	18 C
Warren Way	19 E
Wentworth Clo	19 E
West Walberton La	19 F
Westergate Mews	18 E
Westergate St	18 A
Woodgate Clo	18 A
Woodgate Park	18 A
Woodgate Rd	18 A
Woodside	19 E
Yapton La	19 H
Yapton Rd	19 E

YAPTON

Beagle Dri	20 C
Belmont Ter	20 C
Bilsham Rd	20 B
Blenheim Rd	20 B
Briar Clo	20 B
Burndell Rd	20 C
Canal Rd	20 B
Cherry Av	20 C
Church La	20 B
Church Rd	20 B
Cobham Clo	20 B
Douglas Clo	20 D
Downview Clo	20 C
Downview Rd	20 C
Downview Way	20 C
Drake Dri	20 D
Drove La	20 A
Fairholme Dri	20 C
Ford Industrial Est	20 D
Fordwater Gdns	20 D
Foundry La	20 B
Giles Clo	20 B
Gladstone Rd	20 B
Goodhew Clo	20 C
Graham Rd	20 B
Johnson Way	20 D
Junction Clo	20 D
Loveys Rd	20 B
Main Rd	20 A
Miles Clo	20 D
Mill View Rd	20 B
Mustang Clo	20 D
North End Rd	20 B
Park Dri	20 C
Park Rd	20 C
Rollaston Pk	20 D
St Marys Meadow	20 B
Sproule Clo	20 D
Tack Lee Rd	20 B
The Croft	20 B
The Limes	20 C
The Pines	20 B
The Poplars	20 B
West View Rd	20 B
Yapton Rd	20 E